Slain in the Spirit

"fact or fiction"

Slain in the Spirit

"fact or fiction"

Ezra Coppin

NEW LEAF PRESS

Box 1045 Harrison, Ark 72601

Printed in the United States of America.

Library of Congress Catalog Card Number 75-36001
ISBN: 0-89221-010-9

CONTENTS

AUTHOR'S NOTE

This small work is not intended to be more than an encouragement to those whose minds have been concerned with the scripturality of the experience of these days in which people are so made aware of the person of the Holy Spirit that they "fall under the power." It is my belief, however, that the truths shown me by the Lord in Revelation 1:10-17 have been validly expressed herein. I have no argument with any who disagree, and my longing is that the worldwide movement of the Spirit of God may continue without any contention until Jesus comes.

INTRODUCTION

During my last year in College, I took a course in Western Expansion During the 18th and 19th Centuries. Because I was a pastor, the professor suggested I choose a term paper theme in the line of my work. We settled on the theme *Revivals on the Frontier*. It was a thrilling research and has benefited me much in the years since.

One factor stood out clearly in my study. In every great movement of God in the United States, the actions of the Spirit were distinguished by some form of physical manifestation. In almost every case, the manifestations were evident signs that the power of God had fallen.

Down through church history, and particularly during the past two centuries, the spiritual leaders of the major denominations have sought to explain this fact. Sometimes it has been called mass hysteria; in more modern times, psychological and emotional stress. Indeed it has frequently been called everything but what it normally is—the sign of the presence of the Lord. It would seem, however, that in a very basic sense men have erred in trying to explain the unexplainable. God cannot be explained, only experienced. He is not so easily defined that His beautiful acts can be submitted to the scientific formula, or to the rationalizations of the mind and intellect. It is a tragedy that in seeking to explain divine manifestations away many have succeeded in keeping them away! This has robbed much of professing Christendom of the necessary spiritual attitudes through which the Holy Spirit can reveal Himself.

There is nothing new about being "in the Spirit," or "under the power." It was, is and will be a direct manifestation of the presence of God.

Recently it was my privilege to sit and talk with one of the great preachers of the post-World War II era. Rev. Velmer Gardner lives in retirement in San Diego, California. His name is used here by permission. I interviewed this servant of God because he is one of the last of a special group of men. They were saved and baptized in the Holy Spirit as a result of the ministry of an even greater servant of the Lord—Charles S. Price. Of this man Brother Gardner recorded, "He was the greatest Spirit-filled oratorical preacher in the United States in this century." He left his mark for God, and many of the powerful charismatic preachers today hold a very special place in their hearts for him. He went to be with the Lord in 1947.

In his own life story (reprinted in 1972) Charles S. Price told of the time when he was "slain in the Spirit." He did not want to have such an experience, and the more he saw of scores of others coming under the power of God, the less inclined he was towards the manifestation. He asked his friend Dr. Towner, a Spirit-baptized Baptist, "Do I have to go down?!" Dr. Towner replied, "Yes . . . you don't want to, and therefore you will . . ." According to Charles S. Price, when he received the first sign of the power of God he lay on the floor for hours during which time the Holy Spirit burned in and over him. His own account in the book *And Signs Followed* (page 45 of the Logos reprint) would thrill the heart of any reader. From that time, Price was to become one of the most amazing preachers of the full-gospel in the world. His experience characterized his entire ministry.

Velmer Gardner was in many meetings conducted by Charles Price in days when it really cost something to be a preacher of the experience of Pentecost. As Gardner walked down those years with me, he related things that we might all wish to have seen.

Imagine Charles Price praying for *one thousand people in one night*! The prayer-lines almost always were in excess of five hundred persons. Velmer Gardner related, "If there were five hundred prayed for, ninety-five percent would be 'slain in the Spirit' as Price prayed.

"Many times people, I mean a lot of people, fell under the power of God where they stood. In those days they were permitted to remain where they fell until God was through with them. Many times for hours, and when they finally stood to their feet they were covered with the glory of the Lord.

"In my own meetings," Velmer continued, "I have seen the power of God fall on people when no one was there to assist. They would fall so hard that injury would normally be inevitable but I never saw a person even bruised when 'slain in the Spirit.' "

Physical evidence that the power of the Lord was present is not a new thing. I have said that it was normal in the revivals of the Frontier Days, and it has been normal in all ages of redemptive history. It did not begin on

Azusa St. in Los Angeles, nor on the day of Pentecost. It is an inseparable part of God's dealings with men. All Bible students would agree that such evidence was recorded in the Word of God. Blessed are those in whose lives occur such unmistakable proof of the presence of the Holy Spirit.

Whatever the manifestation of the presence of the Lord, it is important to understand it is a sign that God is present. A person is not healed "by falling!"—nor necessarily while under the power of the Lord. Such phenomena are indicators that the Lord is present to act within the faith-level of the individual.

Evangelist Luke wrote the following fascinating words, "And it came about one day that He (Jesus) was teaching . . . and the power of the Lord was present to heal." When the power of God is present there will be evidence of that in the lives of those waiting on Him.

Chapter 1

Personal Experience

Near the end of my last active pastorate within the Southern Baptist Convention, I was asked a question which plainly embarrassed me. It was not that I needed to have been so affected, for I had experienced the baptism in the Holy Spirit, and was rejoicing in Jesus despite the mounting opposition to my ministry. The exchange took place in the home of a lady who had recently arrived in the area, and who had commenced to attend the church. At my first visit it became clear we had a common life in the Spirit, and it was a joy to continue to minister to her with a view to her affiliating herself with the Body.

One afternoon as we sat talking of the life in the Spirit she suddenly confronted me with the question. It was embarrassing only because I did not know what the question meant!

"Pastor, have you ever been slain in the Spirit?" I wasn't about to admit I did not know what she was talking about, and I simply replied I had not been so "slain." The subject changed, and I never could satisfactorily find the answer to my own ignorance. The Spirit was working powerfully in my own life, but His impact upon the congregation was very small. I remember thinking that a little research seemed indicated, but could think of no place where the phenomenon could be witnessed nor anyone to whom I could turn for elucidation.

Some months later the battle lines were drawn and the issue of the Spirit became the focus upon which I left my church. My last message was preached on August 5, 1973, under the title, *He Touched Me,* but the people never heard it. The last sermon they actually heard was on Sunday evening, July 22. The title captioned a defense of my experience in the Spirit — *"The Charismatic Gifts, Southern Baptist Life and You."* Anything I said in the last three messages until my resignation was ignored by the church, and were it not for my own notes even I would not know the areas of my preaching in the final services.

The sermon on the life in the Spirit was an exegesis of the classic chapters regarding the charismata in 1 Corinthians. But these chapters did not contain anything about being "slain in the Spirit!" The Lord was dealing with me in areas of my own awareness, and they were sufficient in themselves to bring my ministry to a close.

I walked out of my own pulpit that Sunday in August, and into the services of Jerry Barnard at the El Cortez Hotel in downtown San Diego. There I found the refuge my bleeding mind needed, and there I witnessed for the first time the thing which due to my ignorance I knew nothing about. I saw men and women suddenly collapse to the floor in some kind of euphoria or trance. To say I was shocked would be a gross understatement. I was dismayed, and not a little disturbed; perhaps disgusted would come nearest to the truth, but I determined that I could endure this weird thing for the joy of the fellowship within the body of believers.

Some weeks later I was privileged to attend my first charismatic clinic. It was held at Melodyland. There I witnessed much of this phenomenon. It no longer threatened me for I had learned to take a strong karate stance when anyone prayed with me. I was not about to succumb to whatever those who were "slain" were affected by; indeed, no one was ever going to push me over onto the floor! At least, not if I could help it! I just knew that the person ministering was using physical compulsion, or conversely the person ministered to was psyching his or her mind into a condition where the phenomenon would take place. Maybe it was a combination of both! I seemed to observe that those who stood boldly for prayer with one leg firmly braced behind the other rarely did this flip, but it troubled me that these would sometimes "freak out" just the same. Then, when I saw that sometimes people fell over onto the floor with no one near them, my whole rationale began to crumble. I did what any sane-thinking Baptist would do—the whole area was hung on a skyhook as something I would have to tolerate if I was going to mix with people who were flowing in the Spirit. I did not wish to experience this thing, but then, I had not progressed beyond the private use of my prayer language, so I did not wish to get involved in what people called "the flow of the gifts." I believed in the gifts, but the Spirit had not enjoyed opportunity to flow through me at this time.

During a visit to Florida I was given a seat

on a bus going to Kathryn Kuhlman's rally in Tampa. I confess to having mixed emotions! I had difficulty in forgetting all I had been told concerning her ministry! Being so new in the flow of the Spirit I had not learned to overcome the social, religious and cultural backgrounds in which I was raised. From the rigors of Plymouth Brethren dogma through the programs of Southern Baptist life, I continued to be the product of my upbringing for a long time.

Now Sister Kuhlman blew my mind completely! I mean everything went out the window. Jesus was walking among the people and healings were taking place everywhere. Somewhere during the rally she paused long enough to talk about "being slain in the Spirit." She commented many asked her to explain this, but that she had not found any adequate explanation. She said, "All I can believe is that our spiritual beings are not wired for God's full power, and when we plug in to that power we just cannot survive it. We are wired for low voltage; God is high voltage through the Holy Spirit."

I watched with awe. An analytical medical doctor came to the platform to inspect the leg of a patient of his who was claiming a miraculous healing. As his foot hit the top step of the stairs something jackknifed his body and he was thrown suddenly back onto the floor. He staggered to his feet and advanced a little more only to hit the deck again. Finally he got as far as the young man and began to inspect the healed leg. Miss Kuhlman asked him for his opinion, and he replied intensely, "I wish I could heal them like that!" —and down he went for the third time.

That night I decided I better take the whole thing off the skyhook and take a closer look at it. This was more emotional than practical. I had little opportunity to minister in those days, and therefore could not anticipate what might happen if I were to pray in the Spirit with a person.

Finally, I was approaching my first day out alone in the ministry of the Spirit. I was to preach both Sunday services at a Christian Center in Covina, California. The Lord blessed in both meetings, and many came for prayer.

It happened after the evening service. One moment I was praying with a lady, the next she was on the floor. I didn't mind that, but the problem was that I was unaware of what had happened! My fingers were barely touching that lady's head, and I was quite ignorant of the fact she was no longer there. I prayed on, and something made me open my eyes. Deep shock came over me. She was lying on the floor with a heavenly radiance on her face, and I was standing with an arm out and nowhere to put it!

I determined to find out whether the Word of God said anything about this, but before I could make up my mind on the issue, I was "slain in the Spirit!"

It all happened at a midnight communion service sponsored by Christian Faith Center in San Diego. A prominent and powerful servant of the Lord was ministering in "the word of knowledge." He called me out of the congregation by name, declaring that the Lord had given him a word for me. I was becoming accustomed to this kind of ministry, and many such words had already been fulfilled in my life. I had even grown spiritually to the point where I welcomed the penetrations of the Spirit through His servants.

"My brother," he said, "I am raising your arms to shoulder height so that they form with your body the shape of the cross." As he did so he intertwined his fingers in mine as my arms were stretched widely. We stood closely. I felt very secure. Was I not firmly standing, and in such a mutual strength-grip that neither of us was going anywhere?

"My brother, the Lord shows me that you have suffered much, and that as your arms are now in the form of a cross, so you will yet suffer more. But it will be of short duration, and afterwards there will be glory."

I never did know what happened. The Spirit of the Lord exploded over me and in me. I could not fall backwards for I was firmly held. The Lord made a believer out of me! A delirium of joy swept over me, all strength left me; Jesus suddenly was matchlessly beautiful. I buckled at the knees and dropped like a sack of wheat. Oh what sweet things Jesus was saying to me as I lay there at His feet! As I rose the brother who ministered immediately spoke to me again.

"I am to place the mark of the Cross on your head as a symbol of the fact that you are now the exclusive property of the Lord."

This time I floated out and away, distantly aware that some hands had gently caught me as I fell backwards.

From this experience I emerged determined to know what the defense for this experience was. I was still biblically oriented, and I longed for truth which was based on the Word. For six months I rested in the experience of Saul of Tarsus as he met the Master on the road to Damascus. Down in the dirt he heard the voice of the Son of God. Later the Holy Spirit revealed the truth expressed in the rest of this book. Thousands must have preached this as a message of sorts. Some may have even gloried in it; some few may have seen what the Spirit showed me, but to me it was new revelation. To me, the message in the rest of these pages is uniquely my own, because the Holy Spirit revealed it to me. When He did, it was all brand new. My prayer is that it will bless each of you who reads it.

Chapter 2

The Phenomenon – old or new?

Our brothers and sisters of the Old Testament age apparently learned some things which later passed into disuse. Of the many fascinating Scripture passages which bear upon the power of the Holy Spirit to bring people under divine power, none is so thrilling to me as the record of the dedication of Solomon's Temple. It is a repeated passage, but for this study I am using the story as it appears in 2 Chronicles 5.

It had been David's desire to build the house of the Lord, but God has told him this would be accomplished by his son after his death (1 Chronicles 28). David had even gone to the extent of amassing materials and supplies, drawing plans and laying the charge to build upon Solomon. Solomon took it all in deep seriousness and built the house for the Lord. The day came when it was all finished and the dedication services were set. It was a great day in Israel.

The dedication services were highlighted by the placing of the Ark of the Covenant *in its place*. The action required the purification and sanctification of the priests as a body. They did not sanctify according to order or course, but as a body (2 Chronicles 5:11). What a day it must have been. *One hundred and twenty* priests stood clean before the Lord blowing their trumpets in *unison* with the singers (vv. 12-13).

A great cry of praise went up to Heaven. For want of more descriptive words, I am going to say that they used a praise formula which was magical in its results: "He (the Lord) is good, for His mercy endureth forever." This is the 26-fold commentary of Psalm 136. Whatever else it did, it released the power and blessing of the Lord upon His people in Solomon's day.

When the priests stood blowing their trumpets—all 120 of them *in unison*, and the singers sang about the goodness and mercy of the Lord, something dynamic occurred.

THE GLORY OF THE LORD FELL

The record is that the glory of the Lord filled the house of God (2 Chron. 5:14)! Solomon's own commentary upon this is found in 6:1. He referred to the Lord's word that He would dwell in the thick cloud— perhaps a reference to Psalm 97:2. It wasn't a little cloud when the people praised the Lord with the words which delighted the heart of God! It was a cloud that *filled* the place; all-pervasive and overpowering. Look at what resulted from the incoming of the presence of the Lord.

"So the priests could not stand to minister because of the cloud" (5:14).

The priests—all 120 of them were slain in the Spirit. If it be objected that this is an unwarranted extension of the text, let my reader turn to 2 Chronicles 7:1-2. It would appear that when the glory of the Lord filled the place, and the priests were unable to stand the blazing intensity of the power of the divine presence, they got out of there. How? I don't know, but in Chapter 7 they are seen to be outside the house of the Lord, and *unable to enter* because of the glory. What did they do? Just kept on praising the Lord with the same power-releasing formula, "He is good; for His

mercy endureth for ever." (2 Chronicles 7:3)
It was glory upon glory for the people of God
that day. The blessing flowed from Heaven in
unbroken sequence, and the priests were so involved in the outflow that they were unable to
carry on their normal functions. For twenty-
two days the power of God lay on the people,
and finally on the twenty-third day Solomon
sent the people home. I imagine they had
spiritual indigestion!

After the people had gone home, the Lord
told Solomon that all his praying was heard.
He told him that He (the Lord) would stay
among the people (7:12). He further in-
structed them that if sin should enter to
destroy the power and fellowship, the people
could restore the lifelines by repentance and
prayer leading to divine forgiveness (7:14).

Many years passed by, and 120 other
people—"priests of royalty" (1 Peter 2:9)
stood before the Lord in an attitude of ex-
pectant prayer. Our precious Lord Jesus, the
Heavenly Ark, was in position; seated at the
right hand of the Father. There was absolute
unity of heart and mind (Acts 2:1). The glory
of the Lord fell and filled the place. The
Promise of the Father was fulfilled. The Holy
Spirit ushered in the Age of Power.

There is nothing new about the power of

God falling upon His people. It was a phenomenon of the divine presence in the dedication of the Temple. I will not dogmatize, but I believe that 120 priests were slain "under the power" that day. I also believe it was a magnificent type or shadow of something that was going to happen long years afterwards. Something that would make the unfettered power of the Lord available to those who wished to avail themselves of it (Acts 1:8).

Chapter 3

Daniel under the Power of God

The book of Daniel has usually been studied as a prophetical work so some beautiful devotional insights have been overlooked. This man of God knew the power of God as few men have known it, and we examine his life for our continued understanding of the results of direct contact with the Lord.

Daniel received many visions from the Lord. Some were easier to take than others. When the Lord appeared to him in visions which were of magnitude, Scripture reveals his physical responses. For example, "My thoughts were greatly alarming me and my face grew pale, but I kept the matter to myself" (Dan.7:28 NASB). The words "my face grew pale" could be literally translated "my brightness was changing upon me!" At this point Daniel was beginning to reel under the power of the revelations he was receiving from God. He had further to go!

At the end of Daniel 8 there is an interesting progression in his reactions. The interpretation of the vision recorded in this chapter was ordered to be taken to Daniel by one who could be none other than the pre-incarnate Son of God. The awesomeness of the order and the identity of the angel commissioned to bring it, once again brought a great fear upon the servant of God. Verses 17 and 18 make clear that in the presence of the power of God Daniel sank into a spiritual trance. Hundreds of years later the Apostle Peter would do the same (Acts 10). In Peter's case the condition resulted in some attitude changes that were to affect the history of the church.

I am not saying that in this trance Daniel was "slain in the Spirit," but I do contend that he was under the power of God at that point. By the time the vision was made known to him, his weakness before the Lord was in an advanced stage. "Then I, Daniel, was exhausted and sick for days. Then I got up and carried on the king's business; but I was astounded at the vision, and there was none to explain it" (8:27, NASB). Daniel's whole person was being affected by the dynamic of the visions and power of the Lord.

He had still further to go!

Daniel 9 is the revelation of the "seventy weeks" determined upon the people of the Lord, and chapter 10 commences by saying that Daniel received "the message and had an understanding of the vision" (v.1, NASB).

Daniel had been fasting in sorrowful prayer for three entire weeks. He wanted to know all there was to know about the visions the Lord had given him. He was willing to pay the price needed for such communication with God. In chapter 10 the progression of the devotional life of Daniel appears to culminate, and here at least we can use the terms "under the power" or "slain in the Spirit."

To understand what happened to Daniel, it is necessary to carefully identify this other messenger who had the responsibility to inform him of the content and meaning of the additional vision.

Daniel was on the banks of "the great river, that is, the Tigris" (10:4). Apparently, as he communed with the Lord he was impelled to open his eyes and look up. A description of the One whom he saw begins with verse 5.

The description will be significant in our later study of the experience of the Apostle John. Daniel said, "I lifted my eyes and looked, and behold, there was a certain man dressed in linen, whose waist was girded with a belt of pure gold of Uphaz. His body also was like beryl, his face had the appearance of lightning, his eyes were like flaming torches, his arms and feet like the gleam of polished bronze, and the sound of his words like the sound of a tumult" (vv. 5-6, NASB). Knowing the identity of this person is understanding why Daniel reacted as he did. Some commentators have thought the messenger was once again the angel Gabriel, but I think this is unlikely. In Daniel 8:16 an unidentified voice commissioned Gabriel. I believe that the One who appeared to Daniel in chapter 10 was the One whose voice was heard on the previous occasion—the eternal Son of God.

Recently as I was studying this point, I was enthralled by the classic work *The Prophet Daniel* by A. C. Gaebelein. His superb reasoning is so within the understanding the Lord has given me that I feel compelled to extensively quote Dr. Gaebelein:

> "The question is who was this 'certain man,' or as it reads literally in Hebrew, 'a man of desires'? . . . A few expositers of this chapter

have taught that it was none other than the
Lord Himself who paid a visit to the Prophet,
just as He came in the form of a Man to
Abraham (Genesis 18). We incline to this view
and believe that the greatly beloved man was
favored with a Theophany ... the evidence that
we have here an appearing of the Son of God
before His incarnation, in the form of a Man, a
great Christophany, is very convincing. Daniel
was blessed as a man greatly beloved with a
manifestation of the Lord of Glory, just as *the
beloved disciple John, over 600 years later, was
likewise permitted to see the same Lord of Glory.*
There is only one difference. Daniel saw Him
before His incarnation and John beheld Him in
the island of Patmos after His death, trium-
phant resurrection and ascension to Glory.
Both, however, are strikingly alike. In
Revelation 1:12-17 we find the manifestation,
which is so much like the one Daniel had on the
river banks of Hiddekel. Anyone comparing
this scripture with Daniel's record of what he
saw must feel convinced that it is one and the
same person. *And there is also a hint in con-
nection with that vision of glory which Saul of Tarsus had on the road to Damascus.* The men that
were with Daniel saw not the vision, but a great
fear came upon them and they fled. The com-
panions of Saul were likewise filled with terror
'hearing a voice, but seeing no man' (Acts 9:7).

The effect of this great manifestation upon
Daniel was the same which happened to John.
'And when I saw him I fell at His feet as dead'
(Rev. 1:17). Daniel was also on his face towards
the ground and his comeliness was turned in
him into corruption. The deep sleep which

overcame him corresponds to the term 'as dead' in John's experience.

What lessons there are for us here . . . . Daniel acted in faith . . . God honored his faith. Then he talked with angels. Visions came to him. Gabriel appeared next and afterwards was sent 'flying swiftly' with a great message to Daniel. And now after Daniel's prayer and fasting, the Lord Himself appeared to the prophet, who had been so faithful. *Thus he went 'from glory to glory.'*

Yet . . . when he comes face to face with the Lord of Glory, *he utterly collapses and sinks into the dust in His Holy and glorious presence. And that is the place which belongs to every saint . . ."* (Author emphasis)

I am in full agreement with Gaebelein's beautiful reasoning. The Lord Jesus Christ made a personal appearance to Daniel, and it was accompanied by the most astonishing physical phenomenon. The similarity to the later experience of John is startling, even extending to the touch of the hand of the Son of God. The passage in Daniel reads: ". . . no strength was left in me, and my natural color turned to a deathly pallor, and I retained no strength. But I heard the sounds of His words, and I fell into a deep sleep on my face . . . and behold, a hand touched me and set me trembling on my hands and knees . . . then this One with human appearance touched me again and strengthened me. And He said, 'O man of high esteem, do not be afraid. Peace be with you; take courage and be courageous'. Now as soon as He spoke to me, I received strength and said,'May my Lord speak, for You have strengthened me' "(10:8-10, 18-19, NASB).

Daniel's confrontation with the Eternal Son of God came at the end of a progressive development in the deeper things of the Lord. It was so great that he fell on his face before the glory before him. On his face, without any physical power, and exposed to the full radiance of the presence of God, he was quite unable to control what was happening. His actions were involuntary, as are all actions when the power of the Lord falls.

Perhaps the most interesting observation of this lovely story is to see the permanent impact it made upon Daniel. When he had been strengthened by the Lord *he was ready to listen and speak*. Later we will see this same result as we consider the lives of others.

From the vantage point of the Old Testament, we approach the New Testament. It was concealed in the Old, as the Old was revealed in the New. We "take the shoes from off our feet, for the ground whereon we tread is holy."

Chapter 4

A normal Sunday

It was the year A.D. 96. The first century of the Christian era was almost closed. The Emperor Domitian carried the purple over the Roman Empire, and persecution was serious against the people of God. These were hard times for those who loved Jesus. Actually, earlier inspired writers had thought that the Second Coming would occur during their lifetimes, and yet He had not come. Only the beloved John was left alive. His fellow apostles had either been martyred or died naturally. John was not having such a good time either, and he was a very old man about ninety years of age.

Some time earlier, the Roman authorities felt that it would be much better to put him somewhere away from the people among whom he labored at Ephesus. There was not much love in the last decade of that century, and the meddling old man kept talking about loving people. In fact, he had written a pastoral letter to the despised Christians telling them that love was the answer. The authorities felt it would be better to get rid of him without arousing too much bitterness among his followers, so they quietly spirited him away to the Isle of Patmos. We do not know why he was ever permitted to leave the island, but later he was returned to Ephesus, and according to the Church Fathers died there in peace about the end of the decade.

During his exile in Patmos, dear old John wrote the book which we call *The Revelation*. It appears to have closed the canon of scripture chronologically and that is fitting, for it begins with and ends with the concept of the coming of the Lord Jesus Christ. The writings were evidently under the mighty unction of the Holy Spirit, and they began to take shape one Sunday morning during John's devotional time.

It was just a normal Sunday. Nothing spectacular, and the phrasing of the Word in Revelation 1:10 suggests that the day was no different than any other "Lord's Day." We can suppose indeed that it was no different than any other day of the week, except that by this time the church was regularly worshiping on the day upon which the Lord rose from the dead (Acts 20:7; 1 Cor. 16:1-2). This would have given the day a special character to John, for it was he who leaned on Jesus' breast at the Last Supper, and was known as the one whom Jesus especially loved. He stood at the Cross to receive very specific instructions from the Lord, and in every way was close to the heart of his Master. We can suppose that even though each Sunday was a normal remembrance to him, the day was also very special. But it was a normal Sunday morning when he began to receive those things from the Lord which he would leave for us through all ages.

There is a kind of assumptive nonchalance about the words, "I was in the Spirit on the Lord's Day!" Almost as though it were ridiculous to think that he would be in any other condition or state.

Now our Brother John had received some dynamic experiences in the Holy Spirit. He was a member of the select group to whom Jesus said, "Receive ye the Holy Spirit" (John 20:22). That must have been a fantastic moment for him, but what really made a believer out of him was the fulfillment of the promise of the Lord in Luke 24:49—repeated in Acts 1:4-8—that he would receive the effusion of the Spirit after the Ascension. John never said much about Pentecost, but he was there, and life "in the Spirit" became the norm for him. Almost sixty-five years later he was still enjoying the flow of the Spirit which began in his baptism in the Holy Spirit at Pentecost.

So, the Sunday we are considering was a continuation of the life he had known for an entire lifetime!

He got up that morning just as any other morning. It is just possible that he said, "Good morning, Lord! Thank you for Jesus who died and rose again for me. Thank you for the Holy Spirit whom He sent down, and who has empowered my life until now with His presence."

Maybe he continued, "Father, this is just another Sunday, but I want it to be in fellowship with You. I open my whole self to the Spirit so that He can make Jesus precious to me." About that time John began to get happy, as the first eight verses of the chapter indicate.

Clearly a beautiful new anointing of the Spirit came down on him. "Old manna" wasn't enough for this brother! He wanted it fresh every morning apparently, but it was just another normal Sunday morning in the life of one of the Lord's servants. I don't think he suspected that 1,800 years later many people would be trying to say that he was having the last experiences "in the Spirit," and that when he died most of the gifts of the Spirit would become unnecessary, null and void. I suspect that John would have asked God to let him live for ever if he had even dreamed that such a perversion was possible!

Nothing happened to John that morning that should not be the most normal thing for every believer. To be "in the Spirit" is not the same thing as "the Spirit in us!" The latter experience is the result of regeneration and faith in Jesus Christ as Savior and Lord—the former is the result of flowing in the Spirit, an experience deriving from the baptism in the Spirit which comes to believers from the risen Lord Jesus as the equipment for our lives.

What happened to John when he got "in the Spirit" that Sunday morning? The Greek tense used in verse 10 is most literally translated, "I *came to be* in (the) Spirit," so it will be exciting to observe what happened to him when he reaffirmed his Pentecostal experience on that *"imperial day"*—as the literal translation expresses.

Chapter 5

What really happens in the Spirit?

Often Christians are prone to think of life in the Spirit as some kind of exclusive experience, but the experience of Brother John indicates that being "in the Spirit" results in some very definite action. In the case of John, the experience resulting from that new anointing on the Sunday in question was crystallized into the four verbs which follow. We will think of each of them individually, but observe as we go the progression involved.

John said he heard — v. 10.

"I came to be in the Spirit on the imperial day, and *heard* behind me a great, loud voice like a trumpet". . . .

An early and certain result of either the

baptism in the Spirit or of a subsequent flow or anointing is readiness to actually hear the voice of the Lord Jesus. Many Christians can rarely detect the voice of the Lord, because they lack the prerequisite experience of being "in the Spirit." People frequently ask the question, "How can I know if it is the Lord who is speaking to me?" The answer is obvious. The person who flows in the spirit is rarely in doubt. Indeed, sometimes the "still small voice" is loud enough to deafen the waiting ear! The vital element of revelation did not disappear with the completion of the canon either! The voice of the Lord is available to every believer who walks in the Spirit. Whatever He says will be within the general framework of Bible doctrines, but to claim that the voice of the Lord does not clearly come to the believer is to impugn the character of God. It is true that the Word of God contains all that is necessary for faith and doctrine, but the experiential element of faith remains to be shared with the believer's heart through the Holy Spirit.

In the first days of my experience in the baptism in the Spirit, I was frequently puzzled by things which the Lord told me to do, but I obeyed. Never once did such inner revelations prove to be out of His will. Many times, only the open ear could have detected the voice. It is this sensitivity that is the first vital ingredient to the Spirit-filled life. The word *hear* occurs over 1,250 times in the Word of God in one form or another. Obviously the Lord puts weight on our ability to hear, and I contend that to those who do not enjoy the Spirit-filled life, hearing is almost impossible. Life is a matter of conjecture, but "in the Spirit" the hearing of the soul and spirit are quickened. What first happens when we move into the Spirit is the desire to hear and the ability to hear.

What John heard was a big, loud voice telling him what to do! Some would contend that this was sufficient, but John was to experience much more before he did what he was told to do. We live in days when many voices clamour to be heard, and the voice of the Evil One attacks us on every side. It is little wonder that Christians are sidetracked into error. It takes nothing short of an experience "in the Spirit" to bring us to where we can rightly hear the sweet voice of the Son of God.

John turned—v. 12

Notice the progression! John got a new anointing in the Holy Spirit that Sunday morning. It wasn't something that just happened either. He planned it that way! Just as we can determine to flow in the Spirit or walk in the flesh, John chose the Spirit-life. When the anointing fell on him, his ears were suddenly opened to hear all that the Lord Jesus wished to say to him. It thrills me to notice that the Spirit prepared him to hear the Lord Jesus, and during His long discussion about the Comforter in John's Gospel that is just the way Jesus said it would be. His work is to make Jesus real, and that's the way John got it!

The power of the Holy Spirit in our lives, makes us sensitive to the word of the Lord, and then inclines our hearts to obedience and action. John *turned.* The presence of the Holy Spirit in our lives always calls for listening and action. The turning was a vital part of the progression which was taking place. It was actual, but it was also symbolic.

Turning away from ourselves and towards the Lord is a costly process, but it is indubitably a part of what the Holy Spirit wants to achieve in us for Jesus. Many Christians never get over the stage of remembering the past. Paul said in his letter to the church in Philippi, "Forgetting those things which are behind, and reaching forth . . . I press towards the mark for the prize of the high calling of God in Christ Jesus" (3:13-14). Christians get hung up on past failures or experiences, or are sure that they know all there is to know, and never quite make the turn the Lord wants of them. They never know what they miss for they never see what they miss!

Turning and self-denial go hand-in-hand. John was saying to the Lord as he turned, "I am willing to do whatever you want me to do." He was turning from the situation where he was to the situation where the Lord wanted him. It must be obvious that these are truths which can be taught from many passages of the New Testament, but that is not the purpose of this book. We observe these things as we move with John through the progression of that Sunday morning in the Spirit-filled experience.

What strange experiences took place when John turned!

He saw—v.12b

John's seeing was very special. Jesus told him to turn around and see *generally,* and when he turned around he saw *specifically.* The progression is clear. John was experiencing a new movement of the Spirit in his life that Sunday morning, and as a result he became sensitive to the voice of the Lord. Newly sensitive, he became obedient to the point where he turned, and in the turning he came face-to-face with the full glory of divine revelation. The new revelations were in two distinct parts, each covered with the verb *saw*.

The first specific picture John saw was the entire revelation. The first actual feature of the revelation was the presence of the seven golden lampstands (v. 12b). The time that John spent on this part of the total picture was short, for in the middle of the lampstands stood the Lord Jesus!

Everything in the center of the view was Jesus. He filled the sharpened spiritual senses of His servant John. Each of the magnificent qualities of His Person call for exegesis, but again, this in not my purpose. Jesus stood in all of His glory.

> He was Perfection.
> He was Purity.
> He was Power.
> He was Persuasion.

He was everything that John could have ever wanted, then or in eternity. For one blinding moment, John saw Jesus through the Spirit, and the summing up of that experience called for the use of the verb *saw* again. In verse 17, John said, "When I saw *Him*" . . . his first view was an overview of the total picture but his last view was the narrowed-down extravaganza of the immaculate and eternal Son of God.

Follow the progression carefully, for to some extent or other, every Christian who enters into the life in the Spirit will experience similar things.

John's new experience in the Spirit that Sunday morning was to change him forever. His ear became open to the voice of ths Lord, and his feet moved in unison with the will of God. As he turned and saw the *general* area of "life in the Spirit," he got such an eyeful that in the blinding glory of the time, everything else faded away, and all he saw was Jesus! Hallelujah!

The baptism in the Spirit, or the "walk in the Spirit" which follows (Gal. 5), inevitably leads to open ears, movements of obedience and a soul which sees the Lord Jesus in all His beauty and radiance.

Beloved saint of God, go with me now into glory itself, and like Paul, learn how you can hear and see things which you can never share in this world nor will share, until you see Jesus face-to-face and bow with adoration. Jesus wants to give you a foretaste of that experience right now (1 Cor. 12).

Chapter 6

Falling under the Power

We come now to the culmination of the experience of that good old man John. We know he had a new anointing in the Spirit, but his first real association with the phenomenon of the power of the Holy Spirit had taken place six decades before. At that time he had his own personal Pentecost, and I am simple enough to believe that from that day he tried to walk each day in the full blessing of it. Apparently he enjoyed "tuning in" on the Lord's Day because for him, perhaps more than for any other of the disciples, the resurrection had meaning in terms of the love-life he had enjoyed with Jesus.

He was blessed that Sunday on the isle of

Patmos, and as full as he could be. I can't prove it, but I am sure he was praying in tongues and singing in the Spirit according to the teachings of the Apostle Paul. But perhaps he was blessed because he was one who was there when this "life in the Spirit" got started. After all, Paul was a sort of Johnnie-come-lately to this good old man!

Can't you just see him? He was probably walking up and down to begin with, as so many of us do as we pray in the Spirit. Then the action started, and the dear brother got into it fast! He heard, turned, saw ... then saw better, and as soon as the glory of the Lord filled him he automatically entered the last phase of the anointing.

John fell as dead—v. 17.

People get all snarled up with words, and semantics seem so important to those who do not know the baptism in the Spirit! I am reminded of an incident which occurred while I was associated with a well-known charismatic body in San Diego County. I was responsible to find a place for the pastors and elders to conduct a leadership retreat. For years before I came into the release in the Spirit I had been engaged in church camping activities in the county, and I assumed that all

I was required to do was give my name to my friends who ran the facilities and set a time when the place was available. One man whom I had known for many years said to me, "Are you the same Ezra Coppin who used to be at . . ." I assured him affirmatively. He wondered how I came to be in such a strange church setting. I patiently explained that the Lord had brought me into the life in the Spirit. His next statement really threw me for a moment. He asked, "Isn't that the place where people get slain in the Spirit?" When I told him that this was not uncommon, he wanted to know what it was, but he was more concerned that the actual term could not be defended biblically. I never got the use of his campground, nor any other in the area.

John uses the phrase *"I fell."* He tells how and where. He was on the Isle of Patmos; it might as easily have been in Ephesus while he was conducting a clinic for the charismatic bishops of Asia Minor, or in his bedroom. It could have been at the El Cortez Hotel, Melodyland, or in Western Avenue Baptist Church to which I belong.

In an actual spiritual sense he was at Jesus' feet, and experientially he was as "dead." The Greek word used here as *fell* connotes "prostration." In case any of my friends who do not believe should agree that anyone *ought* to "prostrate" himself before the Lord Jesus, let me hasten to say that this is the only use of the word in Holy Scripture where it is associated with the idea of being "as dead." This does not carry the connotation of a voluntary worship as is the case in some other places where the word *fell* is used. The definition "as dead" removes this possibility. That's how careful the Holy Spirit is about biblical concepts.

John became so full of the glory of the Lord and the beauty of His person that he just plainly "fell . . . as dead." It is of no consequence to me nor to the Lord whether people talk about being "slain in the Spirit," "under the Power," or "falling under the Power."

One thing I know: It is scriptural and it is beautiful.

What soul ecstasy, what surfeit of glory when Jesus fills the wondering eye. Of what value is the world then? There are such times when the risen Lord wants to make private communication with the soul and spirit of His children, and the only way He can accomplish it is to put them into such condition that they are unable to argue back.

See what happened that day at Patmos to

John. While he lay in a heavenly stupor, a euphoria of such bliss that he was as though already dead, thinking for sure that he was about to enter Heaven's gates, *Jesus both touched him and talked with him.* When Jesus touched him it was to assure him that there was no need to be afraid. Glory to God! Many of the experiences which come to us in the first days of our lives in the Spirit are so different that the lying devil tells us we are in bad shape. Jesus just wants us to be open to the Spirit for anything He wishes to do or bestow. I know many dear Spirit-filled Christians who are robbing themselves of one or more beautiful spiritual bonanzas by allowing that old Serpent to delude them into thinking the experience is not genuine. One thing is for sure, loving and divine persons, one or all, will never allow a Christian to experience anything which is hurtful when it has been asked for scripturally, in faith, and in the name of Jesus (Luke 11:1-13).

But Jesus also talked with John. He said to him, "I an the first and the last; I am He that liveth and *became* dead, and behold, I am alive for evermore." While John lay on the ground as dead, Jesus was simply saying to him, "I put you down here to tell you something. I made you like dead to tell you that I am alive. I am real, John!"

All that went on between the Lord Jesus and John that day is the substance of the Book of Revelation! It lifts Jesus to the highest plane of glory, extols Him as the King of kings and the Lord of lords. Jesus just moved up to John that day and gave him revelation after revelation of Himself. There is no way to beat that!

The phenomenon of "being slain in the Spirit" is scriptural and profitable. During such times, Jesus speaks to the hearts of believers. Far too often we raise such people too quickly, and before the Master is through talking with them.

Recently I was speaking at a Full Gospel Businessmen's Chapter when the Spirit of God gave me the word of knowledge concerning a woman who was in the audience. The word from the Lord was so specific it would have been impossible for any but the indicated person to respond. The lady was in a group of singers visiting the meeting. As she made her way forward her face slowly crumpled and puckered as the Holy Spirit worked within her. Presently she stood before me. I raised my hand to pray with her, and the power of the Lord fell upon her. It had not even been possible for me to place a finger on her head! She collapsed before the Lord. The

Lord then gave me a word of prophecy concerning her. When the word was completed, someone reached down to assist the lady to her feet, but the Holy Spirit witnessed to me saying the work was incomplete. I asked that she be left alone. The tears flowed, and then with the glory of the sun, Jesus lit her up with joy (Rom. 14:17). People commented on the radiance of her face as she walked back to her seat. Later as she sang it was beautiful to see the peace of the Lord Jesus covering her as a mantle.

The time is long past when I questioned this act of God. It can be faked as can any other spiritual experience; the determination is not mine to make. Ultimate responsibility rests between the parties involved, and the Lord keeps the record. Too many people fake too many things! Salvation, holiness, sanctification, power, church loyalty, love for Jesus, stewardship, and even the baptism in the Holy Spirit—all these and other things can be faked. Shall I reject any one of these because of the fakers? *Fakers prove reality!* The genuine is best attested by the counterfeit.

I want to be where John was! I want to be at the feet of the precious Son of God, feeling His touch and hearing His voice—unconscious of all around me until He the lover of my soul is good and through.

The "in Spirit" experience leads to open ears, moving feet, seeing eyes and touched lives. May the Holy Spirit be able to bring us all under His Power and control.

Chapter 7

The Work of
the Enemy

It has been observed that "Satan can and
will imitate everything Jesus can do except
those things which in any way associate themselves with God's redemptive purposes."

It seems necessary to more specifically deal
with this matter in order that the validity and
worth of being "slain in the Spirit" may not be
made a matter of controversy or ridiculed by
those who are confused with the unreal.

Think of some other things.

Truth. As far back as the Garden of Eden,
Satan sought to make truth into a lie. God
said, "The day thou eatest thereof thou shalt
surely die!" Satan said, "Ye shall not surely
die" (Gen. 2:17; 3:4). The eternal enemy of
our souls sought to make our first parents

question the veracity of the word of the Lord. It is still a favorite technique of his. The Word of God is true and the moral and spiritual laws within it are valid, but Satan seeks to place doubt in the human heart regarding the reliability of that word. The Scripture says of itself, "All scripture is given by inspiration of God and is profitable . . ." (2 Tim. 3:16). But Satan's lie is to say that the record is not reliable nor dependable. He wishes to turn the truth into a lie.

Singing, music, and the dance. The Lord has always wanted His children to enjoy the capacities for these natural, creative things. The Old Testament gave early insights into the joy of the Lord's people as they sang and danced before Him. It was good to "clap the hands," and make "joyful noise unto the Lord." Today the devil has captured the world of entertainment with lewd and unwholesome imitations of the joy which is the native preserve of the saints of God. Who dances before the Lord now? One or two brave hearts! Recently I was speaking at a pastor's retreat in Guatemala when the joy of the Lord broke out among His servants. For one and a half hours they danced in the Spirit. There was holy and wholesome worship in everything they did.

But the devil has placed connotations upon the dance which make it difficult for believers to practice it. Rather than be associated with the perversions of the Evil One, the saints of God have withdrawn from these valid expressions of joy and praise. We've been robbed! Robbed by the one who came to "steal and destroy." The diabolic content of modern dancing, the irregularity of contemporary music and the cultic and drug-laden inferences within the songs of this day have made it hard for the believer to use the media which the Lord intended for praise and happiness. I repeat, we have been robbed!

Legitimate sexual expression. The Lord gave the proper use of sexual expression for the joy and consummation of human experience. Paul wrote, "Marriage is honorable and the bed undefiled" (Heb. 13:4), but the devil has rewritten the text to say "Adultery is legitimate and pornography undefiled!" What God made beautiful within the order which He determined, the devil has made promiscuous. The chastity and sanctity with which the Lord clothed the human sex relationship is so grossly perverted that "live and in color" performances seduce the morality, integrity, and sanctity of marriage. These are not wide generalizations incapable of proof. They are parts of the world in which we live—patent and clear for everyone. It is not my purpose to do more than simply show the ways in which the Devil falsifies what God had pre-determined as real and good.

The baptism in the Holy Spirit. Probably no area more than in this sees the perversions of Satan. The perversion begins in the matter of salvation. The New Testament confession of faith was very simple: "Jesus is Lord." That lordship was acquired individually by the exercise of faith in the redemptive work of the Cross. Salvation was the initiation into a glorious and most meaningful life of power and happiness. To those who were the most earnest and devoted of Jesus' first followers He said, "And ye shall receive power after that the Holy Ghost is come upon you, and ye shall be witnesses unto Me" . . . here, there and everywhere! (Acts 1:8) As early as Acts 8 we observe Simon the sorcerer wanting to buy the power with which the apostles had been invested. Peter simply told him he did not have enough money to obtain it! Furthermore, he was told that it was not something that could be bought for money as he had tried to do.

Satan has duped people into thinking that conversion is a change of life-style, a reformation, or some similar adjustment. God said it was a matter of repentance and faith (Acts 20:21).

In the same manner the genuine experience of the baptism in the Holy Spirit is commonly substituted by the devil with a baptism of demonic power. Classes in occult healing are taught in colleges. As the Holy Spirit intensifies His precious work in the end-time work of Christ, the devil is doing the same. He substitutes evil spirit power in the place of Holy Spirit power. Satan can easily give false peace, false security, false hope, riches, health, and power. But he can never give the eternal peace and joy and unction of the Holy Spirit, for this is a sovereign function of the Lord Jesus Christ.

The gifts of the Holy Spirit. Most of the gifts of the Spirit named in 1 Corinthians 12 are imitated by satanic forces. Perhaps none is so frequently imitated as the gift of tongues. This primary and often initial evidence of the baptism of the Holy Spirit can be so easily counterfeited by Satan. The Apostle John admonished his readers to "try the spirits" (1 John 4:1) because already Satan had sent out many false imitators. Now in the end of time, this need is highly accentuated. Evil tongues are spoken in witches' covens, seances, and cultic churches. Interpretations are common and often accurately pointed.

Because of the ability of the Evil One to do this, many true believers in the Lord Jesus Christ intentionally run from the baptism in the Holy Spirit to avoid the false and the demonic. The devil is smart; he knows that the distinguishing line is fine, so once again he has robbed many Christians of the valid power which they need to pursue the walk of faith with God.

Physical phenomenon. Of all the things in the present church renewal Satan is capable of duplicating, "being slain in the Spirit" must rank as one of the most likely.

I have written of the true and wonderful experience of being "under the power," or "slain in the Spirit." This is part of the special distinctive of the ministry of the Holy Spirit in these days. The genuineness of the true experience is incontestable, but the problem arises with those who are either poorly taught regarding it or those who seek an experience-oriented life and present themselves in every possible situation "so they can fall!"

I have watched with concern the growing trend to provide official catchers to gracefully lower the one who falls. When the power of God is upon a man or woman, the last thing needed is someone to help the Holy Spirit do His work. No person has ever been hurt "falling under the power," and the current trend to comfort and ease has almost made "falling" a fad. Even though this book has been a matter of divine conviction to me, I must admit that in my own ministry there are some who follow from place to place in order to "be slain in the Spirit." But let me also say that I believe these people genuinely desire a constant and new touch of the Spirit of God, and frequently their repeated presence for that purpose betrays the fact that *they are not receiving sound and deep biblical teaching in the life of the Spirit.* The tendency toward experience-oriented faith as opposed to "Jesus-as-Lord oriented faith—experience versus the Person—is to be deplored and resisted, especially by the Lord's servants. The children of God must be taught that the devil "prowls around like a roaring lion, seeking someone to devour" (1 Pet. 5:8, NASB).

Love. Jesus said, "By this shall all men know that ye ar My disciples, if ye have love one for another" (John 13:35, NASB). The great proof of the reality of Jesus in our lives is that we express it in a way characteristic of divine persons.

Paul comments in Romans 5:5: "The love

of God is shed abroad in our hearts by the Holy Spirit" Most people are familiar with the common English word "love." If Jesus is Lord in human experience, *agape* love—God's unconditional kind of love—should be the norm. God loves us regardless of whether He approves of our conduct or not.

All other loves are conditional. They depend upon virtue expressed, doctrines tightly held, class structures adhered to, physical beauty of form and figure, and any one of a hundred other contingencies. God loved us when we were unlovely, and He simply asks us to express this same kind of love toward other believers and to the lost who go on hopelessly without Christ.

What has the devil done to this potentially beautiful relationship? He has cast a veil of doubt and suspicion upon those who seek to transparently walk in it. Agape love lets me embrace my brother, tenderly express concern for my sister, and accept another as myself. The devil persists in confusing conditional love with unconditional love, and again we are robbed!

Recently I was ministering personally to a group who had gathered for prayer following a meeting. I placed a hand on a woman's shoulder and with deep "agape" prayed for her deliverance. Later I heard that I was unwise in my conduct towards women when I prayed for them. The devil had robbed someone of the deep agape love which was his right to experience. On another recent occasion, I was leaving a home prayer meeting. Our hostess had been to the hairdresser that day, and she really looked beautiful! As I passed her at the door I commented that her hair looked lovely. Later her husband accused me of making a pass at his wife! He had been robbed by the devil of an "agape" occasion.

Satan has deceived the children of God into thinking that transparent, honest agape is not possible. The devil is a liar and "the father of lies" (John 8:44).

We have been robbed by the chief robber of them all. The fact that the devil perverts, twists, and changes all the things God has for us in no way invalidates them. We must not "be ignorant of his devices" (2 Cor. 2:11).

If Satan twists the truth then we must hold to truth; if Satan warps the beauty of singing and dancing in the Spirit, then we must preserve these rights in purity and holiness; if Satan wants to pervert the beauty of legitimate sexual expression, then we must preserve it with all our strength and mind; if he wants to imitate and ape the baptism in the Holy Spirit with evil spirit baptism, we must ensure that we know the reality of the former; if he wants us to talk the languages of hell, we must insist on those of heaven; if the devil makes us seek experiences in opposition to reality, we must contend for the real.

To be "slain in the Spirit" is a beautiful and biblical experience, but Satan wants us to join a bandwagon of people who just fall for the sake of falling. If Satan desires to make our inter-personal relationships conditional, we should deny him that right. We must love as Jesus loved, not for a moment allowing the beauty of the real agape experience to be lost in the wiles of his ways.

Jesus revealed the purposes of the devil when he said, "The thief comes only to steal, and kill, and destroy." Everything the Lord Jesus wants to do in us and through us will be subject to imitation and counterfeit. The Master also said, "I came that they might have life, and might have it abundantly" (John 10:10, NASB).

We do not turn away from the beautiful experiences of the life in the Holy Spirit because of the devil's counterfeits. Being warned and awake, we seek only those things which spring from Him. Jesus makes it very clear that when our request is honest and genuine, the results will also be genuine. Our heavenly Father does not give stones to eat! (Luke 11:1-13)

Chapter 8

The touch of Power

Some will want to argue that one isolated reference in the New Testament is insufficient to warrant the assertion of a doctrine, and we can sympathize with such thinking. The treatment of the passage in Revelation is according to the manner which the Holy Spirit made it real to the writer, and it seems hardly likely that dear old Brother John was greatly concerned whether he was experiencing an easy-to-define phenomenon any more than the writer is concerned with the same. Certainly the passage gives far more credibility to being "slain in the Spirit" than lesser passages give to many of the things which the orthodox evangelical church has held important through the centuries.

A whimsical thought persists in my mind. It is not very profound, and I would hesitate to advance it as deductive reasoning, but I really cannot help feeling that no Christian was ever hurt by the touch of the Holy Spirit and by "falling" under His power. Even if there were no biblical basis for the phenomenon, it might be contended that since many are strengthened through the experience, it is worth entertaining. I have reasoned, however, that there is such basis, and therefore we ought to praise the Lord Jesus every time a believer is so open to the Lord that the Spirit can explode the person of the Master within.

But there will always be those who question the experiential value of being "slain in the Spirit." It has not been my intention to provide a theological treatise for the consumption of those who enjoy such material. Rather, I have wanted to give simple ideas of inspiration to those who are simple enough to have wanted them. There are other forums on which to debate and argue for those who deem it profitable.

However, not all has been said in this book that needs to be said. It would be appropriate to refer to two other passages of the Word of God which indicate that those who see the Lord Jesus as he really is are certainly going to be made aware of it in a tangible form.

Jesus' Self-revelation

The youthful and tender young man who reclined against the Lord Jesus at the last Supper later witnessed what the "touch of power" meant!

The Garden of Gethsemane was the place chosen by Jesus for one of His rare self-disclosures and it was to be the last before His death. All 600 soldiers—a Roman cohort, accompanying the traitor Judas, had come upon the Master to capture Him and take Him to trial. What happened must have been something to see! Jesus asked whom they sought. When He identified himself, every one of them seems to have hit the ground (John 18:6). Can you imagine 600 men falling backwards like so many dominoes? Row after row, line after line! There is no reason to assume that any remained standing. What happened to these very highly trained soldiers? Rome had no better men, but in this moment they were reduced to impotence at the word of the Son of God.

In Exodus 3, the Eternal God revealed Himself to Moses as the *I AM*. He was to tell the children of Israel that *"I AM hath sent thee"* (v. 14). It was an awesome title of divine power and excellency.

In John 8, Jesus claimed for Himself the title *I AM* (v. 58). The impact of His claim infuriated the Jews so much that they picked up stones with which to stone Him. The literal translation of John 8:59 is "Jesus *was* hidden"—another occasion when His patent deity was exercised. He was not hidden by others, but apparently became invisible. He could have offered no greater proof of what He was claiming. He was the *Eternal I AM*. This is what He said in the Garden of Gethsemane, and the impact was equally dynamic. Six hundred men fell to the ground at His word.

I am not trying to indicate that 600 men were "slain in the Spirit" but I assert with pure evidence that the touch of the Divine Word was enough to bring 600 men "under the power." What really happens when people are genuinely "slain in the Spirit" is that the Holy Spirit reveals Jesus for who He really is, and for what He is. It is quite an experience!

The Lord of Glory

Our Brother Paul, whose experience has been alluded to earlier, cannot be totally ignored in this study.

Perhaps I am simple. I believe he was saved on the Damascus Road, and baptized in the Spirit in the house of Ananias three days later.

His baptism in the Spirit and physical restoration took place at one time. Interestingly, his water baptism followed afterwards. (See Acts 9:1-18.)

What happened on the Damascus Road?

Acts 9:5 gives the key to what occurred. Into the bigoted and arrogant heart of Saul of Tarsus came the blinding insight that *Jesus was the Lord.* Many evangelical Christians are afraid to call the Lord Jesus Christ by His wonderful and saving name, *Jesus.* If I know Jesus at all, it is to know Him as Lord! If I know Him as Lord, I will hear Him say sweetly, "I am Jesus."

The full vision of Jesus as the Lord of Glory was more than Brother Paul—then Sinner Saul—could possibly stand. His earthly wiring was not geared for that kind of revelation. As a lost man, maybe he was on a six-volt system! One moment of the glory of Jesus as Lord got him rewired onto 110-volts. Three days later he plugged into 220-volts!

The lesson is simple to understand. A sight of the risen Lord Jesus in all His glory will cast any person to the ground blinded. Saul of Tarsus was "slain in the Spirit." I have seen many people so "slain" who were not Christians, and the experience had the fabulously glorious result of "making believers" out of them! They rose to a new life.

If the touch of divine power was valid then, it is valid still. There is altogether too much evidence to take any other position. I am tired of people trying to rationalize the Bible away, and relegate thrilling experiences of the Apostolic Era to the first century.

Power is power! Jesus is still Lord, and to those who approach Him in that holy reverential manner, He still is prone to disclose Himself with evidence and physical manifestations.

If you have known the spiritual phenomenon of being "slain in the Spirit" you can rest in the Lord. You were in a safe and scriptural way.

May the Holy Spirit continue to bless the Body of Christ, and compel us to lie "as dead" at His feet in order that we may hear His sweet voice instructing us in His will and intention for our lives. Some glad day soon, we "will walk in Jerusalem, just like John," but until that day we should long for Jerusalem-conditions within our hearts.

Chapter 9

The double Touch

Some time ago I was scheduled to hold meetings in a Canadian city. During the negotiations for the visit, I wrote to the minister of the Anglican Renewal Center asking whether he wished me to visit with his congregation while I was in the city. Along with my letter I sent him copy of the original edition of this work. It was with some dismay that I received his reply. Not only did he not wish to have me in the Center, but frankly expressed his disbelief in such "far out" practices as the book discussed!

Months later when I arrived in that city, my host informed me the vicar had requested a conference with me, the time for which was already arranged. As I sat in the vicar's study, the good brother was somewhat embarrassed. We fenced with one another for a few minutes, but the tension was suddenly broken as he blurted out, "Rev. Coppin, I have asked you to meet me so that I might apologize to you." For what, I wondered. Then he related this story.

Soon after he wrote me, he was invited to the first World Convention of Anglican Charismatics in London. His people had pooled resources to make the trip a reality for him.

While at the convention he was asked to minister at a weekend retreat. At the conclusion of one of the services many came to the altar for prayer—some standing, some kneeling at the altar railing. With true Anglican formality he prayed for them with the "laying on of hands." The first person upon whom he placed his hands fell like a log under the power of God. This was not supposed to happen! One by one those standing were "slain in the Spirit." The vicar was shocked and distressed to see all these people who were "under the power." The dear brother decided that perhaps it would be much better if he prayed for those who were already kneeling at the altar since they were firmly braced with their arms on the railing. He moved to the first, and immediately the power of God fell again, and the kneeling believer slowly went over sideways!

None of this was supposed to happen! But it was happening in the prayer life of one who had refused to accept this demonstration of the power of God.

My brother asked me to forgive him! For what? I praised the Lord with him that God had added this new understanding to his life and ministry.

Earlier I argued that this phenomenon in itself is nothing more than the evidence that "God is present." I contend that people are not necessarily blessed in any other way when this occurs. Healing does not necessarily take place, nor is the baptism in the Spirit an automatic or immediate result. This is the theological fact.

Nevertheless, God does frequently give a double touch of His presence, and it is important for us to see this potentially dynamic manner of His operation. It is important to remember that other works of God occurring simultaneously with being "slain in the Spirit" are in His sovereignty. As I wrestled with this matter the Lord brought to my attention that when a Christian is "under the power" there is complete surrender of all personal pride and arrogancy. The Spirit of God impressed on me that these additional touches *can and do take place because "self" is in the place where it no longer hinders the work of God!*

The following "case histories" are all known personally to me. It would be possible to compile whole books of such cases, but the Lord has indicated those about whom He wishes me to speak.

Slain in the Spirit accompanied by new power

Recently I was one of about a hundred ministers present in a Morris Cerullo meeting in Pasadena, California. The Lord led His servant to first minister to the preachers. There was holy confusion as one hundred men were "slain under the Spirit." While the preachers lay prostrate before God, Cerullo called for those in the congregation who had never received the baptism of the Spirit to come *to* the platform, for, he said, "These men will minister with new power!"

Never in my life have I seen anything like what happened in the next hour. People streamed to the platform where one hundred preachers waited like "lions of God." Cerullo was correct! Those men would have turned Los Angeles upside down if they had ministered in their churches as they did on that platform. Scores of people received the in-filling of the Holy Spirit at the least touch from those newly anointed hands. Somewhere in the middle of that Pentecost I gathered my thoughts together long enough to realize what had happened. One hundred men came to that rostrum, tired with the burdens of the pastoral ministry; weary with the cares of others and many of them probably at the end of their spiritual rope. One hundred men received a new touch of power as they were "slain in the Spirit." They lay like logs all over the plat-form. As the Holy Spirit blessed each man, the cares and burdens were all taken, the frustrations of the day relieved, and the minds all cleared of the adhesions of the secular world. Thus they were able to minister in the power and glory of the Lord.

Slain in the Spirit with the baptism of power
As the preachers placed those newly anointed hands on those who came, the first evidence of the continued presence of God was the fact that almost all who were ministered to were immediately "slain in the Spirit." It was a "holocaust"—I use the word carefully for Webster defines *holocaust* in the primary sense as "an offering the whole of which is burned; a burned offering." In the lives of those who

streamed towards the platform with simple faith, a great burning took place! The Spirit slew them, then burned through and through. Many rose from the floor praising the Lord in tongues—with the languages of heaven, needing no one to touch them further nor to pray with them. Glory to God! Heaven touched earth!

Roy Tuttle lives in Romoland, Calif. Everybody in the village knows Roy. For years he had sought the baptism of the Spirit, but because "he loved to watch" it seemed that he never got down to the serious business of his own need. In the 1975 World Convention of the Full Gospel Businessmen he came under conviction that it was time for him to seek the power of the Lord. He went home determined that although he was nearer seventy than sixty he would ask the Lord to fill him with Holy Spirit power.

Roy was present at a breakfast meeting of men in Redlands, Calif. when he decided that he would ask for special prayer. What happened to Roy Tuttle is a classic example of the touch of divine power associated with being slain in the Spirit.

A young and relatively inexperienced preacher-boy was ministering to those who had come for prayer. The young preacher

prayed for Roy with the "laying on of hands."
A great and terrible shaking possessed Roy's
body, and he was suddenly thrown backwards
by the power of God to lie on the floor in a
spiritual trance. The rudiments of a heavenly
language came to him, but the incredible fact
was that he was filled with such power in the
Spirit that five days later he was still reeling
around like a "drunk man" (Acts 2:15). So
great was the power of God in him that the
mere mention of the name of Jesus once again
brought him "under the power." Roy's life
was instantly and permanently changed. Now
he goes everywhere joyfully witnessing for the
Lord. He sings "in the Spirit," while he drives
his car, and it all happened when he was
"slain in the Spirit."

Recently I was in Auckland, New Zealand,
having lunch with some friends who were
resident students in the Bible School conducted by Rob Wheeler. We were sharing
together the ways of the Spirit. Someone in the
party commented about the phenomenon of
being "slain in the Spirit." The young married
son of my friends immediately gave testimony
that when he was "slain in the Spirit" he
received the baptism of the Spirit with the
evidence of heavenly languages. It would have
been hard to have persuaded him that this experience was not from God!

Slain in the Spirit for special commissioning
God took action in Grover C. Sinsley's life,
which introduces another dimension to the
phenomenon of "being slain in the Spirit."

Brother Sinsley's secretary came to work
one day in great distress. Her sister had been
involved in a serious motorcycle accident.
"Mr. Sinsley," she said, "Gloria may die. She
is in a coma, and may never come out of it.
We need a miracle!"

It was the second Friday of June, 1972,
when Grover went to a prayer service to in-
tercede for the injured girl. With a deep bur-
den in his soul he prayed, "Lord, I ask you to
heal this girl." He made his way slowly to the
altar, seeking faith to believe for the young
woman who was at the point of death with a
severe concussion, internal bleeding, a broken
wrist, and multiple contusions. The coma had
deepened. Still Grover sought healing for her,
and as he brought the need before the church,
the pastor prayed for him first. He passed into
a deep trance as he was "slain in the Spirit."
Fifteen to twenty minutes later he rose from
the floor, "having been greatly ministered to
by the Holy Spirit."

In the period when Grover was entranced
before the Lord, *He received instructions to go*

*to the hospital and lay hands on Gloria to pray
for her healing, with the assurance that she would
be healed!*

At the hospital, the doctor told him that
even if Gloria came out of the coma, it would
be at least two years before she could be ex-
pected to talk or walk. But Grover had his instructions. On the Saturday after his commission he prayed for Gloria and laid hands
upon her in the name of the Lord—not doub-
ting. On Sunday, Gloria broke out of the coma
and was talking and laughing with her family.
On Wednesday night she slept normally, and
when she awoke on Thursday morning, every
evidence of her accident had gone. The internal bleeding had stopped, the contusions
had all gone, the massive concussion could not
be detected at all, and the broken wrist was
totally healed. Even the ghastly black eye that
disfigured her face had gone. Jesus had completely restored her.

The commission for this prayer of faith had
been received as the Holy Spirit ministered to
Grover's spirit during the time he had been
"slain in the Spirit."

The following story was related to me by a
man who witnessed the incident.

During the Prayer-and-Share-Hour one
Thursday morning at the Christian Center in

Anaheim, a ten-year-old girl was "slain in the Spirit." After fifteen minutes in a deep trance the ministering pastors began to feel some concern. After the service she was carried to the prayer room for special care. One of the leading brothers at Melodyland continued to minister to her until finally she re-entered earth's environment from the spiritual outer-space to which she had gone.

When the girl revived, she looked around her in surprise, and said, "Where is He?" Those in the room immediately asked her, "Where is whom?" The child replied, "Jesus. I was talking with Him, and He told me that if I went to the nursery and prayed for my little brother He would heal him."

The ministering brothers took her to the nursery where she placed her hands on her sick brother and he was immediately healed as the Lord had promised her in the commission she received when "under the power of the Spirit."

Slain in the Spirit for deliverance
During Nora Lam's first visit to the Palm Springs Full Gospel Businessmen's Chapter meeting a notable miracle took place when a young man was slain before the Lord. The young man was possessed with a spirit of

alcoholism. He was slightly inebriated, and "smelled like a brewery." On the night of Nora's ministry, God was doing great works and miracles among younger people. This particular young man finally rose from the floor, completely sober, speaking in tongues (he received the baptism of the Spirit simultaneously, and delivered from alcohol even the smell of beer gone from him and from his clothes. Brother Gerrard related, "He was really praising the Lord. That a miracle had come to him was very obvious to us all."

A personal friend of mine testifies of being completely delivered from a deep-seated grudge when she was "slain in the Spirit." She had presented herself before the Lord with a desire to be free from the hate which was eroding her Christian life. She remembers nothing after she was prayed for until she came to while lying on her back on the floor. In the place of the grudge and hatred had come a compassion and love for the person she had hated.

Pedro Ruiz is currently involved in evangelistic endeavor for the Lord. He related his own story to me:

"All of my life I hated old people. I wanted to say to them, 'Why don't you just drop dead and get out of our way. It's a young person's world'." Pedro thought a moment as he spoke and then continued. "Brother, when I got up from the floor can you guess what was the first thing I did? I rushed to the first old lady near me and threw my arms around her and told her I loved her. There has never been an age gap for me since then. I was freed of hatred for older people."

Those who have received complete inner healings when "slain in the Spirit" are too numerous to mention. In this area especially, God erases the past and enables the believer to rise to a new joy and peace. Forgiveness seems natural when people are "slain in the Spirit."

One of the most beautiful stories concerning the experience of "being slain in the Spirit" comes from a well-known attorney. George's life was one big mess. He was on the verge of bankruptcy. His marriage was on the rocks and a divorce was driving him and his wife onwards. There was not one area of his life in which there was a ray of sunshine or hope. In desperation he came before the Lord for special prayer. He knew that he needed deliverance from demonic oppression.

Down on the floor while he was tuned in to the divine wave length, the Holy Spirit spoke to him.

"George, I am baptizing you in my great

power. You will receive the full flow of my gifts. Your marriage will be healed, and your finances will be restored."

When George was earth-oriented again, he staggered out of the building incapable of fully comprehending all that the Lord had said. *But is happened as the Lord had said!* When George talked with me, he said he would welcome any person who wished to talk with him. What a testimony. I wondered and marveled at the power of God that could take the analytical mind of an attorney and reduce it to the simplicity of faith.

In San Diego, California one of the Lord's servants called out a handsome young man through the word of knowledge. The evangelist told him, "You are a skeptic and will not believe." The young man admitted this was the truth. Some time later he got off the floor praising the Lord in heavenly languages and delivered from the demons of doubt. He told the evangelist that his father was a movie producer in Hollywood who was currently making a film which made a mockery of divine healing!

One of the most thrilling stories in my files is that given to me by Dr. Thomas Miller, pastor of Trinity Community Church.

He entered the services of Angelus Temple

(headquarters of the Foursquare Churches International) as a skeptical modernist. Aimee Semple McPherson was still a great power for God.

At nine o'clock one morning Dr. Miller was "slain in the Spirit" and lay on his back until 5:00 P.M.! Eight hours! Dr. Miller did not believe one basic fundamental doctrine of the Scripture. When the Spirit of the Lord was through with him that day and sent him back to the world of men, everything had become different. He now believed in the incarnation, the deity of the Lord Jesus Christ, the vicarious atonement, the resurrection, and the second coming of Christ. From that day he began to preach the whole gospel—Jesus as Savior, Baptizer, Healer and Coming King!
" When I was first slain in the Spirit I was delivered from doubt demons regarding the flow of the gifts of the Spirit. I became a whole believer in a whole gospel!"

Slain in the Spirit for healing
Physical healing is often associated with the phenomenon of being "slain in the Spirit." Each "case" presented here exalts Jesus as Lord, but some are especially thrilling to the believing heart.

In San Bernardino there occurred an almost

incredible miracle healing. A young man from Colton was attending a tent meeting where the evangelist was moving profoundly in the word of knowledge. He called the case of a young man who was present with a serious bleeding ulcer and who had taken many aspirin in an effort to gain enough relief to attend. From out of the congregation came a young Phillipino to stand before the Lord.

The evangelist did a most unorthodox thing. Turning towards the man, he hit him with a tremendous blow in the pit of his stomach. His closed fist doubled the man over, and he flew through the air and then he lay still. The evangelist laughed with victory and said, "I had to do what the Lord told me to do—hit him where the pain was! Don't worry about him, God is healing him under the power of the Spirit." When the man got up he rushed to the evangelist and threw his arms around him, praising the Lord that his pain was gone. He was indeed healed.

A person who witnessed this mighty act went over to sit with the healed man and asked, "Did you feel the evangelist's punch when he hit you?"

"Did he really hit me," he answered. "All I felt was a blinding light. I went down, and when I got up I was healed."

Out of the ministry of John Spoon come two amazing stories. In August, 1975, John was holding a special meeting on Beardstown, Ill. A close relative, Emmitt Mayes, who was afflicted with heart disease, attended the meetings. Emmitt was "slain in the Spirit" and was so long in a spiritual trance that argument broke out with John's aunt. John said to her, "Aunt Mayes, you may be my aunt, and that may be my Uncle Emmitt, but in the name of Jesus I command you to leave him alone. God is healing him right now."

Next day Uncle Emmitt went to the doctor, who in absolute amazement told him that there was now nothing wrong with his heart. The impact of this sensational episode was so great in the town that another relative, Uncle Fred, came to the meetings. Fred figured that if God could heal Emmitt in the shape he was, "He can surely heal me!" Fred had chronic migraine headaches and stomach troubles. In the first meeting Fred attended he was "slain"—and he was healed as he lay before the Lord.

Brother Jim Spillman of Omega Fellowship, as a traditional and conservative Baptist pastor, used to have some very firm views about people and things. For instance, he believed that all "Pentecostalists" were crazy and guilty of serious theological error. He believed Kathryn Kuhlman was a witch! He thought the baptism in the Spirit, tongues, and other manifestations of the Spirit were demonic. To Jim education was power, and he had much education.

Somehow he was trapped into attending a Kathryn Kuhlman rally. He hid out in a far balcony. The balcony disgorged him as the whale disgorged Johah, for Miss Kuhlman called a special healing for ulcers in a balcony—where he was alone! Finally an attendant brought him to the platform, and as his feet stood on the top of the steps, the power of God took Pastor Spillman and leveled him on his back.

Now nothing made sense to Jim! He didn't believe in divine healing but they said he was healed; he did not believe in Kathryn but there stood Kathryn; he did not believe in being "slain in the Spirit," but now he was lying on his back in a spiritual euphoria, in the presence of many people. Jim relates that he wanted to stay there forever, for great waves of power and glory were rolling over him. His ulcers were healed immediately; his life was changed, he entered into the life of the Holy Spirit and now today is out in the vanguard of those who are carrying the thrust of the end-time ministry of the Lord Jesus.

Most southern Californians who move in the life of the Holy Spirit know "Wild Bill" and Mrs. Monteith. Their story of being "slain in the Spirit" is too beautiful to leave out of this book. "Wild Bill" was also a deep-dyed Baptist, and there were some things he just would not accept after he received the baptism of the Holy Spirit. I imagine that all "us Baptists" have needed to come the same arduous pathway. "Wild Bill" was all for the power of the Spirit, but wanted no part of the business of being "slain in the Spirit."

Bill was a sick man. During World War II his back had been injured, and now twenty-eight years later he was still suffering. Two or three times each year he went into traction, and was never out of pain. In August, 1972, "Wild Bill" decided that God was going to heal him, and he presented himself before the Lord for prayer at that time. As he stood with others waiting for Rev. Fred Price to pray for him, he consciously braced himself and positioned his feet so that nothing could push him over. Bill surely had something to learn, because when Fred Price got to Bill's neighbor, the power of God fell so heavily on that man that the spill-over dumped on Bill. Brother Price never got to Bill! He was down and out—long gone!

"Wild Bill" was tamed! The Spirit of God took him on a glory-ride, and when it was all over he rose to his feet completely healed. There has been not one twinge of pain since and no need for hospitalization. God made a believer out of "Wild Bill" also. A year later Brother Spillman was ministering to "Wild Bill" and his wife at a convention in Ventura. Mrs. Monteith had never been "slain in the Spirit," but on this occasion both went under the power of God together. While they were prostrate before God, the Holy Spirit spoke to Mrs. Monteith saying, "I will take away your husband's job and security. His resources will finish. I will be his supply from now, and you shall both serve the Lord Jesus together." And so it happened within a few months.

Bob Widener was dying of leukemia when the Lord met him in the experience of being "slain in the Spirit." He decided to attend the services of Melodyland Christian Center one Thursday morning. He knew God was going to heal him—he waited in vain! The Lord did not lead Dr. Wilkerson to call a healing for leukemia. Bob was puzzled. He just sat in his place when the service was over. The devil had him buffaloed into thinking that unless Pastor Wilkerson called the healing he could not be healed. Many dear people have been robbed this way, for God wants our eyes to be turned to Jesus.

Following the service, an elder approached Bob to ask why he was still there and so obviously distressed. Bob told him. The elder suggested they go down to the altar right then and ask God to heal the blood condition. Bob was immediately "slain in the Spirit." He lay a long time before God, and apparently while he was prone in his body and spirit, the Holy Spirit ministered Jesus to his body. He knew he was healed because of the strength that came into his body. Blood tests that week left the doctors dumbfounded. Bob *was* healed. Every last trace of leukemia had disappeared.

In the movement of the Holy Spirit today, the phenomenon of being "slain in the Spirit" or "under the power" is seen more and more. The true act of the Spirit is *demonstration* not *exhibition*. I have contended that this phenomenon happens primarily in order for God to get the attention of the person; it is God saying, "I am here."

My earnest prayer is that all God's children will realize that there can be a *double touch*. God is sovereign, and if He can ever get us to listen and be still before Him, there is no limit to what He can do.